Returning to Benjamin
Victor Burgin

DISCOURSE 008

Returning to Benjamin
Victor Burgin

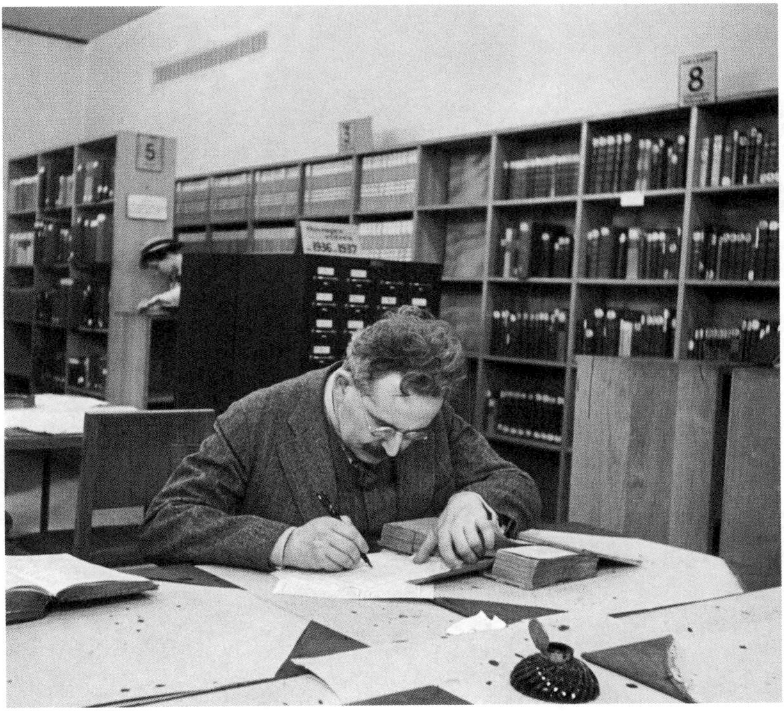

Walter Benjamin at work in the Bibliothèque Nationale, Paris, 1935

Walter Benjamin's 1935 essay 'The Work of Art in the Age of Mechanical Reproduction' has become a classic text. The novelist Italo Calvino defines a 'classic' text as one to which one *returns* – one which you never really finish reading.[1] I first read Benjamin's 'The Work of Art' essay in 1970 when it appeared in English translation in *Illuminations,* the Jonathan Cape edition of a 1955 collection of Benjamin's writings by the German publisher Suhrkamp, with an introduction by Hannah Arendt. I returned to it most recently in the 2008 Harvard translation of Benjamin's 1936 version of the essay, the one Benjamin himself considered definitive. Seven manuscript pages longer than the Jonathan Cape text, and now titled 'The Work of Art in the Age of Its Technological Reproducibility', this is the version to which I shall refer in what follows. Most recently Suhrkamp has published a volume devoted entirely to 'The Work of Art in the Age of Its Technological Reproducibility'. It includes five distinct versions of the essay and related manuscripts dating from 1935 to 1940, together with four hundred pages of commentary. I am not a Benjamin specialist and do not pretend to add to the already vast field of Benjamin scholarship. I intend to revisit 'The Work of Art' essay in the spirit in which Benjamin proposes we approach all history. In 1940, in his last completed essay, he famously writes: 'To articulate the past historically does not mean to recognize it "the way it really was". It means to seize hold of a memory as it flashes up at a moment of danger.'[2] I shall not try to say what Benjamin's classic text 'really was' but rather to say what it suggests to me when I view it today through a prism of present concerns. In this perspective, three interrelated topics appear to me most salient: *democratisation*, *technology*, and *medium*.

Democratisation

To begin with what is already well known, in 'The Work of Art in the Age of Its Technological Reproducibility', Walter Benjamin considers how our relation to works of art changes once we can mechanically reproduce them. He uses the term 'aura' to refer to a quality of a work that is lost or transformed when the work no longer exists only as a singular and unique object. As if in compensation for the loss of aura, however, there is the newly acquired ability of the individual to, in a sense, 'possess' the work, and make their own use of it. For example, he writes: 'The cathedral leaves its site to be received in the studio of an art lover; the choral work performed in an auditorium or in the open air is enjoyed in a private room.'[3]

The French novelist and Gaullist government minister André Malraux celebrates this consequence of reproduction in his 1947 book *Museum Without Walls* (*Le Musée Imaginaire*). For Malraux, photographic reproduction allows individuals to construct their own 'imaginary museum', their own ideal art collection derived from all art works across the globe and from all times. Benjamin however places his emphasis not on the individual but on the collective. The aura of the Mona Lisa places the viewer who stands before the painting in the Louvre in a relation of quasi-religious veneration which isolates them from a relation with others around them. When disseminated through reproduction, however, the image *de facto* addresses a collectivity, thereby potentially contributing to the democratisation of art. More importantly for Benjamin, though, democratisation is seen as affecting not only the reception of works of art but their production. He writes: 'The distinction between author and public is about to lose its axiomatic character ... At any moment, the reader is ready to become a writer'.[4] In the Soviet Union, writers belonging to the Proletkult organisation had given classes to factory workers with the intention that workers would not only read newspapers and novels but also write them. In Germany the *Arbeiter-Fotograf* movement was a comparable initiative that aimed to teach photography and filmmaking skills to workers so that they themselves might represent their own lives.

Although Benjamin speaks briefly about photography in the artwork essay it is primarily cinema that he sees as a potentially revolutionary force – whether produced by the proletariat themselves or by such leftist artists as Charles Chaplin and Bertolt Brecht. That Benjamin's optimism was nevertheless tempered by doubt is apparent in a footnote in which he remarks: 'What is revealed in recent Disney films was latent in some of the earlier ones: the cosy acceptance of bestiality and violence as inevitable concomitants of existence.'[5] This doubt was shared by his friend and interlocutor Theodor Adorno. In a 1936 letter to Benjamin written in response to 'The Work of Art' essay, Adorno writes: 'The idea that a reactionary individual can be transformed into a member of the avant-garde through an intimate acquaintance with the films of Chaplin, strikes me as simple romanticization.'[6]

Adorno and his Frankfurt School associates subsequently hardened their assessment of industrial mass culture. In their 1947 essay 'The Culture Industry: Enlightenment and Mass Deception', Adorno and Max Horkheimer analyse mass culture as a mechanism for enforcing conformity through pleasure. By the final quarter of the twentieth century, the revolutionary class consciousness in which Brecht and Benjamin had placed their hopes had largely dissipated. In common with such intellectuals before him, the Italian writer and film director Pier Paolo Pasolini had first viewed the condition and culture of the poor as a source of vitality for the revolution to come, only to then witness the post-war assimilation of the heterogeneity of popular culture to a uniform, mediatic mass culture. In 1975 he writes:

> I have seen 'with my own eyes' behaviour imposed by the power of consumerism remodel and deform the consciousness of the Italian people, to the point of an irreversible degradation; which did not happen during Fascist fascism, a period during which behaviour was totally dissociated from consciousness.[7]

Movements such as Arbeiter-Fotograf in Germany and Proletkult in the Soviet Union sought to put the means of visual and written representation into the hands of workers, thereby erasing the bourgeois category 'artist' from the pages of history. In an irony of history such ambitions have since been realised not by revolutionary organisation but by capitalist innovation. Digital image technologies now allow for practices based on the historic example of cinema, but with amateur and professional artists enjoying almost equal access to the means of production and distribution. This has not, however, achieved the political transformation of society for which these movements had hoped. At the time Benjamin wrote, the world was divided between two oppositional ideological blocks, capitalism and communism. But the means of reconciling the two was already emerging. In his 1928 book *Propaganda*, Edward Bernays, pioneer of the American publicity industry, writes: 'The conscious and intelligent manipulation of the organized habits and opinions of the masses is an important element in democratic society.'[8] Along these lines, he writes,

> A single factory, potentially capable of supplying a whole continent with its particular produce, cannot afford to wait until the public asks for its product; it

> must maintain constant touch, through advertising and propaganda, with the vast public in order to assure itself the continuous demand which alone will make its costly plant profitable.[9]

Today, the devastating cost to the environment of the credo of boundless industrial production need not be argued. Nevertheless, as the American intellectual historian and Benjamin scholar Susan Buck-Morss remarks:

> Industrial production has not … abated. Commodities are still produced, marketed, desired, consumed, and thrown away – in more areas of the globe, and in greater quantities than ever. Consumerism, far from on the wane, has penetrated the last socialist bastion of mainland China to become, arguably, the first global ideological form.[10]

Technology

The political optimism with which Benjamin could view the mechanical reproduction of works of art was part of a wider hope that industrialisation in general would bring about an egalitarian society free from want. Such optimism did not survive into the later years of the twentieth century. Writing in 1995, Buck-Morss observes:

> A certain kind of industrial dreamworld has dissipated, one that dominated the political imagination in both East and West for most of the century. To be sure, in the East the dream-form was a utopia of production, whereas in the West it was a utopia of consumption. But both shared intimately the optimistic vision of a mass society beyond material scarcity, and the collective, social goal, through massive industrial construction, of transforming the natural world.[11]

Doubts in respect to the project of transforming nature through technology, however, were expressed long before industrial modernity. Around 300 BCE, the Chinese philosopher Zhuangzi imagined a confrontation between a disciple of Confucius and a Daoist gardener. Having watched the gardener labouring with a rudimentary and inefficient means of watering his plants, the Confucian informs him that a machine exists that can water a hundred fields in a day with much less effort. The gardener replies that whoever uses such a machine will have a mind like a machine, and that whoever views the world with such a mind will lose oneness with the world.

In *The Freudian Robot* (2010) Lydia H. Liu remarks on the appearance of this ancient parable in the writings of the quantum physicist Werner Heisenberg, the philosopher Martin Heidegger, and the media theorist Marshall McLuhan. In his 1953 lecture 'The Picture of Nature in Contemporary Physics', Heisenberg cites the story as evidence that existential and ethical questions about the human use of technology are nothing new but have been with us since the beginning of recorded history. McLuhan repeats the Chinese parable in *Understanding Media*, 1964, paying tribute to Heisenberg for '[pointing] out that technical change alters not only habits of life, but patterns of thought and valuation'.[12]

Heidegger's essay 'The Question Concerning Technology' (1953) was written in response to Heisenberg's lecture. Heidegger argues that in its Presocratic Greek origins, the idea of *tékhnē* (craft) is intimately allied to *epistēmē* (knowledge) and *poiēsis* (art), and that technology was originally conceived as a way of understanding nature, not of dominating it. Modern technology, however, has come to treat nature as what Heidegger calls a 'standing reserve' (*Bestand*) of resources to be exploited, with human beings incorporated into the same system as 'human resources' for this same reserve. This is what he calls 'enframing' (*Gestell*) – a view of the world that categorises, quantifies, and entabulates in order to control and instrumentalise. Heidegger writes: 'Enframing means that way of revealing which holds sway in the essence of modern technology and which is itself nothing technological.'[13] What Heidegger opposes therefore is not technology as such, but rather a technocratic understanding of what it is to be human.

Like Heidegger, the French philosopher Gilbert Simondon sees the technocratically enframed mindset of Western modernity as originating in the Aristotelian doctrine of 'hylomorphism', according to which all existing things result from the imposition of a form upon inert matter.[14] Aristotle gives the example of a brick, which results from the imposition of the shape of a wooden mould on clay. Simondon objects that this purely abstract picture leaves out everything essential in the actual production of the brick. The mould cannot impose its form on any matter whatsoever, nor can the clay lend itself to just any form; they are in a sense preadapted to each other. When wet clay is thrown into the mould the wood resists the impact as if 'pushing back' – there is reciprocal action, rather than an active/passive relation. Simondon finds such interdependencies and exchanges at play throughout the production of Aristotle's brick, from the molecular level up to the system of slave labour.

Heidegger accepts the hylomorphic model while rejecting its application beyond the sphere of technological production; Simondon rejects the model itself. In his book *On the Mode of Existence of Technical Objects* (1958) he argues – in a view which receives empirical support in the work of the French palaeontologist André Leroi-Gourhan – that technology is not something added to an already-existing human being. Rather, it was only through technology that 'humans' *came into being*. Leroi-Gourhan writes: 'Tools and skeletons evolved synchronously'.[15] Rather than alienating the human from the rest of the natural world, technology mediates between the two; technologies are part of the way of life of the culture that produces them. Whereas Heidegger urges the necessity of maintaining an aesthetico-sacred space alongside technology, Simondon argues that the technical object itself has a role in culture – one equal to that of the aesthetic object or the sacred object. He charges that Western philosophy has nevertheless largely ignored technology, and as a result is incapable of understanding either the mode of existence of technical objects or our condition of being in a world increasingly occupied and shaped by them.

We may today confirm the terrible prescience of an observation Walter Benjamin made over a century ago. In his

1921 essay 'Capitalism as Religion', he writes: 'Capitalism is entirely without precedent, in that it is a religion which offers not the reform of existence but its complete destruction.'[16] The rapacious and unrestrained instrumentalisation of nature as a 'standing reserve' has led to the decimation of some human populations and the annihilation of many non-human species; it has ravaged terrestrial habitats and poisoned the oceans. A popular 1973 BBC television series charting the history of civilisation was called, with patriarchal unselfconsciousness, *The Ascent of Man*. The world of the ineluctable 'ascent of man' – a world conceived as a standing reserve of inexhaustible abundance – is now definitively past, although many remain who disavow this. In a recent television interview, the French sociologist and philosopher of science Bruno Latour observes:

> We speak of inhabiting the Earth. But we don't inhabit the Earth, we inhabit a thin crust of surface, about ten kilometres thick, which we share with other living beings – four billion years of organisms interacting with each other to produce the conditions that we find habitable. Industrialised humans have had a disproportionate impact upon the habitability of this zone. We are in lockdown in this critical zone.[17]

According to Latour, it was at the suggestion of the novelist William Golding that the British physiologist and engineer James Lovelock named this critical zone 'Gaia', the name given in Greek antiquity to the Earth Goddess. For the Greeks however Gaia was very far from the benevolent and nourishing 'Mother Earth' of later sentimental fantasy. 'Gaia' names the implacable blind force of nature – a nature now responding to the interventions of modern 'man' with no concern whatsoever that the human species survive the response.

Bruno Latour is known as a contributor to 'actor-network theory'. The word 'actor' here can refer not only to a human being but also to any other thing whatsoever, whether animate or inanimate; it can also refer to such abstract entities as concepts and beliefs. Latour has given the example of the 1986 Space Shuttle Challenger disaster. At first sight the shuttle might appear as a coherently delineated independent object endowed with the capacity to launch into space. But in the aftermath of the catastrophic accident, it was shown to comprise a heterogeneous multitude of entities: physical hardware, computer software, management practices, government policies, and so on. What had appeared to sight as a self-contained object was revealed as a previously invisible shifting network of disparate actors, all contributing in greater or lesser degree to the eventual failure of two seals in a rocket booster joint – leading the Presidential Commission that inquired into the disaster to conclude that it was 'an accident rooted in history'.[18]

The perspective of actor-network theory may already be found in Simondon's work. For Simondon, a technical object, whether a space shuttle or a spinning top, is defined through an account of its position in a network of relations which he calls its 'associated milieu'. I have cited his account of the network of actors that compose Aristotle's clay brick. In another example, Simondon writes: 'The technicity of the automobile does not lie entirely in the automobile object; it consists in its adaptive correspondence to the travelled environment, through the intermediary network of roads.'[19]

An 'automobile object' moving down a road has physical substance, but what kind of historically unprecedented 'object' travels across the Internet?[20] The Hong Kong philosopher of technology Yuk Hui aims to account for this 'digital object' – significantly different from that described by Simondon in that it has no material substance. In his

2016 book *On the Existence of Digital Objects*, Hui writes: 'By digital objects, I mean objects that take shape on a screen … composed of data and metadata regulated by structures or schemas.'[21] A fire-breathing dragon in a videogame, the gamer's medical records on a hospital computer, the Wikipedia entry for 'Hospital', are all digital objects.[22] Unlike the objects of philosophical enquiry that preceded it, the digital object is immaterial, but it is not the *only* immaterial object. Among other immaterial objects is the *psychical object*. The dragon on the gamer's screen is a component of the gamer's psychical reality, one that elapses in synchrony with their consciousness as their avatar does battle with it. The philosopher of science Anne-Françoise Schmid says, 'We need a concept of the object … which takes account of the intentions or projections on or in the object.'[23]

If we are to consider the totality of intentions or projections in the case of the automobile object, we must therefore consider, amongst other things, the dimension of fantasy in the *desire* to drive – as expressed, for example, in the cinematic genre of the 'road movie'. From the perspective of actor-network theory (albeit no doubt beyond the Presidential remit), the Challenger Shuttle inquiry might in principle have accounted for the fantasies that nourish the project of space flight. Material things are not the only reality. What psychoanalysis calls 'psychical reality' also has real effects. German Chancellor Angela Merkel, in common with other European politicians, believed that to become energy-dependent on Russia was the best way of guaranteeing peace with her neighbour. No place was allocated in this market-minded calculation for the agency of the fantasy of 'Greater Russia'.

A form of critical attention that disaggregates its object into a rhizomic field of interdependencies is nowhere better exemplified than in Benjamin's work. In this network diagram plan for his 1931 essay on the Austrian writer Karl Krauss, interrelated thematic keywords spawn dependent sub-categories, which in turn prompt cascading annotations, emphases, and erasures.

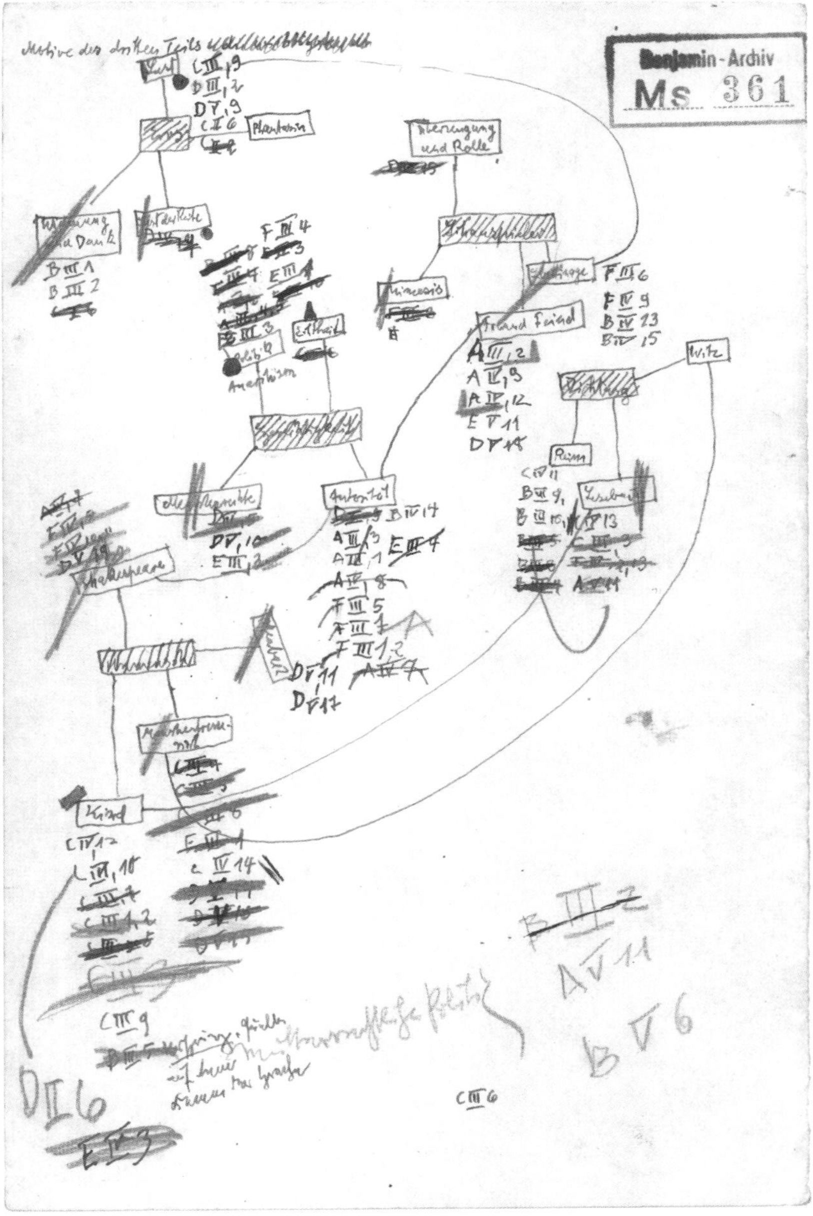
Motive des dritten Teils
Benjamin-Archiv
Ms 361
C III, 9
D III, 2
D V, 9
C II 6
Phantasie
Überzeugung und Rolle
B III 1
B III 2
F III 4
E III 4
B III 3
Ethik
F III 6
F IV 9
B IV 13
B IV 15
Mimesis
Freund Feind
A III, 2
A IV, 3
A IV, 12
E V 11
Witz
Raum
Autorität
B IV 14
D V, 10
E III, 2
Shakespeare
A III, 3
A III, 1
F III 5
F III 1, 2
D V, 11
D V 17
B III 9
Kind
C IV, 12
C IV 14
C III 9
A V 11
B V 6
C III 6
D II 6

Medium

The German media scholar Tobias Wilke has observed that although Benjamin's writings on technology are widely credited with inaugurating modern media studies, Benjamin himself hardly ever speaks of medium. Wilke notes that the word 'medium' occurs only twice in the artwork essay, and the plural form 'media' not at all. One occurrence of the word nevertheless clearly indicates that Benjamin uses the term in a radically different sense from that habitually given to it today. He writes:

> Just as the entire mode of existence of human collectives changes over long historical periods, so too does the mode of perception. The way in which human perception is organised – the medium in which it occurs – is conditioned not only by nature but by history.[24]

Wilke comments: 'The 'medium historical' analysis so brilliantly performed by Benjamin's essay is therefore not only, and perhaps not even primarily, concerned with the technological questions upon which later, more apparatus-centred models of media history have tended to focus.'[25] Benjamin assimilates the idea of 'medium' to 'the way in which human perception is organised'. In 'The Work of Art' he argues that the technologies of film and photography reveal what had previously been invisible. He writes:

> With the close-up, space expands; with slow motion, movement is extended … Clearly, it is another nature which speaks to the camera as compared to the eye. 'Other', above all in the sense that a space informed by human consciousness gives way to a space informed by the unconscious … It is through the camera that we first

discover the optical unconscious, just as we discover the instinctual unconscious through psychoanalysis.[26]

The French philosopher of the image Marie-José Mondzain observes: 'There is no culture of looking that is not a culture of the invisible at the heart of visibility itself.'[27] In revisiting Benjamin's essay we might ask, following Mondzain, what invisibility digital technologies may now be revealing – but with the important rider to which Mondzain alerts us: to 'reveal' the invisible is not necessarily to make a *thing* visible. More fundamentally it is to trace the determinations in everyday life of *that which we cannot see*, of that which – like the psychoanalytic unconscious – acts on us without our conscious awareness. We might think of these determinations as the counterparts in the cultural sphere of such invisibilities as were revealed by Newtonian and quantum physics, by bacteriology and virology.

In 1985 the French philosopher Jean-François Lyotard curated an exhibition at the Centre Georges Pompidou, Paris, in which he sought to articulate the contribution to the 'postmodern condition' of what he called 'telecommunication technologies'. The title he gave to the exhibition was 'The Immaterials' (*Les Immatériaux*). He writes: 'Prisoners of the materialism of industrial revolution, the immaterial materials suffer from their invisibility.'[28] Today, in the aftermath of the digital revolution, we are still largely 'prisoners of the materialism of the industrial revolution'. This is evident from, among other things, academic critical theory. The second half of the twentieth century saw an expansion of what has become generally known as 'visual cultural studies': from Art History, through Film Studies, then Photography Studies, and most recently Digital Media. An effect of digital technologies however has been to challenge the primacy of 'medium' implied in the widely used appellation 'Digital Media'. In 1986, as the first digital cameras were arriving on the consumer market, the German media theorist Friederich A. Kittler wrote:

> Once optical fiber networks turn formerly distinct data flows into a standardized series of digitized numbers, any medium can be translated into any other … a digital base will erase the very concept of medium.[29]

Without Kittler's prescience, participants in the 'indexicality' debate that greeted the arrival of digital cameras misinterpreted the signs of the revolution to come.[30] The real revolution in photography came not with the arrival of cameras with digital sensors but rather with the broadband connection of these cameras to the Internet, where the information they produced merged with the universal field of 'big data'.

In the 1930s Walter Benjamin saw the arrival of cinema as accompanied by a demand for the invention of the concepts that would be required in order to understand the new regimes of the image that cinema would bring. An analogous demand may be felt today in relation to the products of digital image technologies. But whereas in Benjamin's day 'cinema' named a circumscribed and relatively homogeneous institutional and aesthetic *object*, what we may provisionally call 'digital image practices' now present a heterogeneous and boundless technological and phenomenological *field*. If an object of study is nevertheless to be discerned within this field it can only be through a fundamental revision of what constitutes an object.

The most ubiquitously visible manifestation of this object is the *screen*. The film theorist Vivian Sobchack urges that we 'go beyond thinking about screens as discrete devices with different forms, functions, and contents, and attempt to describe the "screenness" that grounds and connects them all'.[31] I would further recommend that, beyond the materiality of such devices, we take account of 'screenness' in all its aspects. As the film theorists Dominique Chateau and José Moure write: 'The screen could be considered to be material, mental or, more generally, a link between matter and mind.'[32]

In confronting the screened real of representations today we do not immediately confront the discrete objects of media studies, but rather the type of object formulated in recent work in epistemology and philosophy of science. In a rudimentary and opportunistic appropriation of the technical complexities of such work, two basic procedural tenets may be extracted: a *flat ontology* – that is, a non-hierarchical attitude to phenomenologically given things;[33] and a definition of the 'complex object' made of these things to include the intention of the observer – what Anne-Françoise Schmid calls a *contemporary object*.[34] Schmid suggests that we 'treat this object as a kind of unknown 'X', the properties of which are distributed in an unprecedented way between different disciplinary forms of knowledge. An object with multiple dimensions, each of which is a discipline'.[35] This is not to be understood as a familiar call for 'interdisciplinarity'. In a co-authored paper of 2011, Schmid and her collaborators write: 'It is no longer a matter of "passing" a given object from one discipline to another … but of constructing an object whose dimensions are themselves disciplinary, which we call an "integrative object".'[36] An 'integrative object' is one 'which no longer [opposes] subject and object across a phenomenological divide.'[37] This conception of the object – consistent with Benjamin's assimilation of 'medium' to 'the way in which human perception is organised', to Simondon's 'associated milieu', and to actor-network theory – offers a radical alternative to what Wilke characterises as 'apparatus-centred models of media history'.

Returning

In the mid-1930s, Walter Benjamin posed the question of the relation of art to the dominant representational technologies of his time: photography and film. To return to the artwork essay today in the spirit in which it was written is to ask the same question in respect of the hegemonic representational technology of our own time: the digital. Benjamin found that the medium of photography and film had dissolved the auratic quality of art. Digital technology has dissolved the very category of 'medium' itself. The hegemony of digital technology, unlike that of film and photography, is not bound by material substance and is therefore without limit. In a 1964 lecture Martin Heidegger predicted that 'cybernetics' would dissolve even the category of philosophy as it colonised all facets of human life and the natural world. He says: 'Cybernetics transforms language into an exchange of messages. The arts become regulated-regulating instruments of information.'[38]

A 'message' in cybernetics has no meaning; it has a logical syntax but no semantics. In Lacanian terms I might say it has no *imaginary* dimension. Although pessimistic, Heidegger nevertheless appeals to the arts, and to visual art in particular, for the potential they may yet retain for representing ethical and non-instrumental ways of being in the world. Yuk Hui returns to Heidegger's question of the relations between art and technology in his 2021 book *Art and Cosmotechnics*. In agreement with Simondon, Hui does not follow Heidegger in viewing art in *opposition* to technology. He rather sees art as potentially intervening *within* technology to combat the reduction of technology to a means of capitalist extraction. However, as a reviewer of Hui's book observes: '*Art and*

Cosmotechnics… spills little ink reflecting on what this sort of artistic process might look like.'[39]

Heidegger's friend and biographer Heinrich Petzet describes how toward the end of his life Heidegger made several journeys to Provence to see the country that Cézanne had painted, and especially the Sainte-Victoire mountain, the subject of about eighty works by the artist. Petzet writes: 'In his old age, Heidegger frequently said that Cézanne's path was his own path – a statement whose full significance has not yet been grasped.'[40] Although Hui offers a detailed analysis of Heidegger's interest in such modernist painters as Cézanne and Paul Klee, and additionally refers to classical Chinese landscape painting, he offers little indication of what a present art form might be that engages technology in the way he envisages. In the absence of examples, one may look to historical precedents. As I wrote in a 2002 article:

> The late 1960s saw such initiatives as 'Experiments in Art and Technology' (EAT) in the US, and the 'Cybernetic Serendipity' exhibition at the ICA, London, presaging current computer-based convergences between art and technology … In an essay published in 1980, the art historian and critic Jack Burnham, who was closely involved in the major art and technology projects of the late 1960s, gives a retrospective account of his own experience of EAT: 'While EAT and other art groups held out the boon of "new discoveries" to corporations funding them, most companies were cynical and wise enough to realize that the research abilities of nearly all artists are nil.'[41]

As John Beck and Ryan Bishop have shown in panoramic detail in their 2020 book *Technocrats of the Imagination: Art, Technology, and the Military-industrial Avant-garde*, such initiatives as EAT were far from hostile to the broader cultural climate of mid-century corporate liberalism.[42] I do not believe, however, that an adequate alternative to such collaborationism lies either in technophobia or in the pious ambition to 'humanise' technology – as if technology were not already fully human. For the philosopher of technology Bernard Stiegler, for example, every technology is a *pharmakon*. An element of toxicity accompanies any benefits it may bring.[43]

Stiegler was amongst the earliest to signal the threat that the information technology industry poses for democratic institutions. Apart from such now widely discussed practices as personal data harvesting and election manipulation, we may cite the information industry's expansion into the neoliberal marketisation of education in what Stiegler calls 'algorithmic governmentality'. I face this each time I open my university e-mail. I used to have colleagues; now I have 'team-mates'. The very words we use to address each other have been taken from our mouths and handed to Microsoft for conversion into management-speak.

As much as we speak language, language speaks us. Language is a machine and we are all caught in the gears. In the Chinese parable, the Daoist gardener warns that whoever uses a machine will think like the machine. This is what Lydia H. Liu means by 'Freudian robot'. In a 2011 interview she explains:

> I define the Freudian robot as 'any networked being who embodies the feedback loop of human-machine simulacra and cannot free her/him/itself from the cybernetic unconscious.' Call it a cyborg, android, or posthuman, the lines between robots and humans are getting increasingly blurred. Just as robots are built to resemble humans more and more closely, humans think and behave more and more like robots. I believe this

> can tell us something about our co-evolution with the technologies we invent and, ultimately, what human civilization is all about.[44]

'The Work of Art in the Age of Its Technological Reproducibility' addresses what human civilization is all about. It is a political essay, but it is not a political tract. It encourages us to think, it does not tell us what to think. To return to the essay today is to face the problem and responsibility of defining what constitutes a politics of art in our present conjuncture. Contrary to what one might suppose if one read no further than the title of his essay, Benjamin does not simply set out to situate a pregiven 'art' in its relation to technology. Rather, he sees that changes in technology may change the very concept of art. He therefore sets out to overhaul the categories of thought within which art had previously been conceived. This is likewise the aim elaborated in his 1934 essay 'The Author as Producer', in which he indicts self-defining 'left-wing' writers who produce 'entertainment literature' about the plight of the working class, and photographers who '[succeed] in transforming even abject poverty … into an object of enjoyment.'[45]

For Benjamin, the political meaning of a work of art does not reside in its overt content – too often an expression of the moral narcissism of its author. It derives more fundamentally from the artist's ability to question the conditions within which art is produced, which Brecht gave the name 'apparatus'.[46] The concept of apparatus has since been elaborated by other writers, most notably by Michel Foucault. In questions put to him in 1977 following the publication of the first volume of his *History of Sexuality*, Foucault was asked to explain what he meant by the word 'apparatus' (*dispositif*) when speaking of the 'apparatus of sexuality'. He replies:

> Firstly, a thoroughly heterogeneous ensemble consisting of discourses, institutions, architectural forms, regulatory decisions, laws, administrative measures, scientific statements, philosophical, moral, and philanthropic propositions … the said as much as the unsaid. Such are the elements of the apparatus. The apparatus itself is the system of relations that can be established between these elements.[47]

Such a definition chimes with a rhizomic critical perspective in which the objects 'art' and 'technology' disaggregate to provisionally coalesce as more-or-less contingent partial objects, 'objects with multiple dimensions'. In his 2008 book *What Is an Apparatus?* the Italian philosopher Giorgio Agamben tracks the source of Foucault's idea of apparatus to Heidegger's 'enframing' and offers his own succinct definition. He writes:

> I call *apparatus* all of that which has, in one way or another, the capacity to capture, orient, determine, intercept, model, control and guarantee the gestures, conduct, opinions and discourse of living beings.[48]

In a 2018 newspaper article the French philosopher and art historian Georges Didi-Huberman voices what is probably a universal sentiment. Our everyday world, he notes, is flooded with images competing to capture our attention, but 'they are so numerous, omnipresent, and put on the same level (*mises en équivalence*), that we no longer really look at them: it is too much, one can no longer keep up, the eye drowns'.[49] He concludes: 'Let us speak no more of images in general, even less of the image in the absolute: let us speak of the uses that, here or there, we can, we must, make of them … [for] in the final analysis, the imagination is the political faculty par excellence.'[50] In 'The Work of Art in the Age of Its Technological Reproducibility' Walter

Benjamin speaks of the necessity of forging concepts that are 'completely useless for the purposes of fascism.' We might consider analogously the necessity of producing ideas and artworks that are completely useless for the purposes of material and human exploitation. We might then paraphrase Didi-Huberman and say 'let us speak no more of technology in general, even less of technology in the absolute: let us speak of the uses that, here or there, we can, we must, make of it … [for] in the final analysis, the imagination is the political faculty par excellence'.

In the classical myth, Procrustes was an innkeeper who had beds of a single size. If a guest was too short, he would stretch them to fit; if too tall he would cut them down to size. We are increasingly required to fit ourselves to a 'enframed' world in which what is not quantifiable and cannot be monetised is not valued – a world in which success is measured in decimal points through rankings and league tables of institutions and individuals. In his own 1992 meditation on the relation between art and technology, the French psychoanalyst and philosopher Félix Guattari writes:

> The contemporary world … is incapable of absorbing, in a way compatible with the interests of humanity, the extraordinary technico-scientific mutations which are convulsing it. It is locked in a vertiginous race towards either ruin or radical renewal. All compasses – economic, social, political, moral, traditional – have become disoriented, one after the other. It therefore becomes imperative to re-establish the axes of value, the fundamental finalities of human relations … An ecology of the virtual is therefore just as urgent as the ecologies of the visible world.[51]

Talk given for Winchester School of Art, Faculty of Arts & Humanities, University of Southampton, 4 July 2022.

Notes

1 Italo Calvino, 'Why Read the Classics', *The New York Review* (9 October 1986), https://www.nybooks.com/articles/1986/10/09/why-read-the-classics/

2 Walter Benjamin, 'Theses on the Philosophy of History', in *Illuminations,* ed. Hannah Arendt, trans. Harry Zohn (London: Jonathan Cape, 1970), p. 257.

3 Walter Benjamin, 'The Work of Art in the Age of Its Technological Reproducibility: Second Version', in *The Work of Art in the Age of Its Technological Reproducibility and Other Writings on Media*, ed. Michael Jennings, Brigid Doherty, and Thomas Levin, trans. E.F.N. Jephcott, Rodney Livingstone, Howard Eiland, and others (Cambridge, Mass.: The Belknap Press of Harvard University Press, 2008), p. 22.

4 Benjamin, 'The Work of Art in the Age of Its Technological Reproducibility', pp. 33–4.

5 Benjamin, 'The Work of Art in the Age of Its Technological Reproducibility', pp. 51–2, n. 29.

6 Theodor Adorno, Letter of 18 March 1936, in *Theodor W. Adorno and Walter Benjamin: The Complete Correspondence 1928–1940*, ed. Henri Lonitz, trans. Nicholas Walker (Cambridge, Mass.: Harvard University Press, 1999), p. 130.

7 Pier Paolo Pasolini, 'Le vide du pouvoir en Italie', *Corriere della sera*, 1 February, 1975. Collected in *Écrits corsaires*, trans. Philippe Guilhon (Paris: Flammarion, 1976), pp. 185 (my translation).

8 Edward L. Bernays, *Propaganda* (1928), History is a Weapon, http://history isaweapon.com/defcon1/bernprop.html

9 Bernays, *Propaganda.*

10 Susan Buck-Morss, 'Preface', *Dreamworld and Catastrophe: The Passing of Mass Utopia in East and West*, (Cambridge, Mass. and London: MIT Press, 2000), p. ix.

11 Susan Buck-Morss, 'The City as Dreamworld and Catastrophe', *October* 73 (Summer 1995), p. 3. She notes that 'fascism, too, shared in this mass utopian dream'.

12 Marshall McLuhan, *Understanding Media: The Extensions of Man* (New York: McGraw-Hill, 1964), p. 63.

13 Martin Heidegger, *The Question Concerning Technology and Other Essays*, trans. William Lovitt (New York: Harper & Row Publishers, Inc., 1977), p. 20.

14 Hylemorphism (or 'hylomorphism') from 'matter' (*hyle*) and 'form' (*morphe*). The argument summarized in this passage can be found in Gilbert Simondon, *On the Mode of Existence of Technical Objects*, trans. Cécile Malaspina and John Rogove (Minneapolis: Univocal Publishing, 2017), pp. 247–62. First published in French as *Du mode d'existence des objets techniques* (Paris: Flammarion, 1958).

15 André Leroi-Gourhan, *Gesture and Speech*, trans. Anna Bostock Berger (Cambridge, Mass.: MIT Press, 1993), p. 97. As cited in Bernard Stiegler,

Technics and Time, 1: The Fault of Epimetheus (Stanford, Calif.: Stanford University, 1998), p. 154.

16 Walter Benjamin·'Capitalism as Religion' (1921) in *Selected Writings Vol. 1, 1913–1926* (Cambridge, Mass.: The Belknap Press of Harvard University Press, 1996), p. 289.

17 Bruno Latour, 'Interview with Bruno Latour', https://www.arte.tv/en/videos/106738-001-A/interview-with-bruno-latour/

18 Presidential commission on the Space Shuttle Challenger Accident, *Report to the President by the Presidential Commission on the Space Shuttle Challenger Accident* (Washington, DC: US Presidential Commission, 1986). The phrase was the title of the report's sixth chapter.

19 Gilbert Simondon, 'Culture and Technics' (1965), *Radical Philosophy* 189 (Jan/Feb 2015), p. 22.

20 Gilbert Simondon died in 1989, four years before the release of the Mosaic web browser that first allowed users to view images from within the browser without first downloading them as separate files.

21 Yuk Hui, *On the Existence of Digital Objects* (Minneapolis: University of Minnesota, 2016), p. 1.

22 Albeit of different types. Respectively, they exemplify the two basic forms of digitization that Yuk Hui terms 'mapping' and 'tagging'. See Hui, *On the Existence of Digital Objects*, p. 50.

23 Anne-Françoise Schmid, 'On Contemporary Objects', in *Simulation, Exercise, Operations*, ed. Robin Mackay (Falmouth: Urbanomic, 2015), pp. 65.

24 Benjamin, 'The Work of Art in the Age of Its Technological Reproducibility', p. 23.

25 Tobias Wilke, 'Tacti(ca)lity Reclaimed: Benjamin's Medium, the Avant-Garde, and the Politics of the Senses', *Grey Room* 39 (Spring 2010), p. 41.

26 Walter Benjamin, 'The Work of Art in the Age of Its Technological Reproducibility', p. 37.

27 Marie-José Mondzain, *Confiscation: Des mots, des images et du temps* (Paris: Les liens qui libèrent, 2017), p. 45 (my translation).

28 Jean-François Lyotard, *Les Immatériaux* (Paris: Centre Georges Pompidou, 1985), p. 16. Curated by Lyotard and Thierry Chaput, the exhibition was held from 8 March to 15 July 1985.

29 Friederich A. Kittler, *Gramophone, Film, Typewriter* (1986), trans. Geoffrey Winthrop-Young and Michael Wutz (Stanford, Calif.: Stanford University, 1999), pp. 1–2.

30 The preoccupation with 'medium' is a characteristic of modernist aesthetics from Clement Greenberg to Rosalind Krauss; see my essay, '"Medium" and "Specificity"', in *Photography Theory*, ed. James Elkins (New York: Routledge, 2006), pp. 363–69.

31 Vivian Sobchack, 'From Screen-Scape to Screen-Sphere: A Mediation in Media Res', in *Screens: From Materiality to Spectatorship: A Historical and*

Theoretical Reassessment, ed. Dominique Chateau and José Moure (Amsterdam: Amsterdam University, 2016), p. 162.

32 Dominique Chateau and José Moure, 'Introduction: Screen, a Concept in Progress', in *Screens: From Materiality to Spectatorship*, p. 17.

33 For example, the French philosopher and novelist Tristan Garcia writes: 'We live in this world of things, where a cutting of acacia, a gene, a computer-generated image, a transplantable hand, a musical sample, a trademarked name, or a sexual service are comparable things.' See Garcia, *Form and Object: A Treatise on Things* (2010) (Edinburgh: Edinburgh University, 2014), p. 1.

34 I assume Schmid's term alludes to Edmund Husserl's notion of the 'contemporary object' as one that elapses in synchrony with apprehension of it. Husserl gives the example of a melody.

35 Anne-Françoise Schmid, 'On Contemporary Objects', in *Simulation, Exercise, Operations*, ed. Robin Mackay (Falmouth: Urbanomic, 2015), pp. 65–6. Schmid continues: 'This is the way designers and inventors think: Not by seeing the object as the result of a disciplinary rationality, even a composite one, but by putting an unknown 'X' in relation with islands of knowledge that cannot all be foreseen in advance.'

36 Anne-Françoise Schmid, Muriel Mambrini-Doudet, Armand Hatchuel, 'Une nouvelle logique de l'interdisciplinarité', *Nouvelles perspectives en science social*, 7:1 (October 2011), p. 115.

37 Anne-Françoise Schmid, 'On Contemporary Objects', p. 65.

38 Martin Heidegger, 'The End of Philosophy and the Task of Thinking', in *Discourse on Thinking* (1966) (New York: Harper and Row, 1977), p. 376. I have modified the translation. The English text renders Heidegger's *Nachrichten* as 'news'. See p. 72 of 'Das ende der Philosophie und die Aufgabe des Denkens', at http://laboratoirefig.fr/wp-content/uploads/2016/04/Pages-de-Heidegger-Gesamtausgabe-14-Zur-sache-des-denkens-.pdf

39 Bryan Norton, 'Technology After Hegemony: On Yuk Hui's "Art and Cosmo technics"', *Los Angeles Review of Books*, 2 April 2022, https://lareview ofbooks.org/article/technology-after-hegemony-on-yuk-huis-art-and-cosmotechnics/

40 Heinrich Wiegand Petzet, *Encounters and Dialogues with Martin Heidegger 1929–1976* (Chicago: University of Chicago Press, 1993), p. 132.

41 Victor Burgin, 'Thoughts on "research" degrees in visual arts departments' [2002], *Journal of Media Practice*, 7:2 (2006), pp. 101–08. I quote Jack Burnham, 'Art and Technology: The Panacea That Failed', in *Video Culture: A Critical Investigation*, ed. John Hanhardt (Rochester: Visual Studies Workshop, 1986), p. 243.

42 John Beck and Ryan Bishop, *Technocrats of the Imagination: Art, Technology, and the Military-industrial Avant-garde* (Chapel Hill: Duke University Press, 2020).

43 Stiegler borrows *pharmakon* from Plato via Derrida.

44 'Lydia H. Liu on her book *The Freudian Robot: Digital Media and the Future of the Unconscious*', ROROTKO, 12 June 2011, http://rorotoko.com/inter view/20110615_liu_lydia_freudian_robot_digital_media_future_unconscious/

45 Walter Benjamin, 'The Author as Producer', in *Selected Writings Vol. 2: 1927–1934,* ed. Michael Jennings, Howard Eiland and Gary Smith, trans. Rodney Livingstone and others (Cambridge, Mass.: The Belknap Press of Harvard University Press, 1999), p. 775.

46 Bertolt Brecht, 'The Modern Theatre is Epic Theatre', in *Brecht on Theatre: The Development of an Aesthetic*, ed. and trans. John Willett (London: Methuen and Co., 1964), p. 34.

47 'The Confession of the Flesh', in Michel Foucault*, Power/Knowledge: Selected Interviews and Other Writings*, ed. Colin Gordon (Brighton: The Harvester Press, 1980), p. 194.

48 Giorgio Agamben, *Qu'est-ce qu'un dispositif?* (Dijon-Quetigny: Rivages poche, 2008), p. 31 (my translation).

49 Georges Didi-Huberman, 'Images-pouvoirs ou images-désirs?', *Le Monde*, 5 October 2018, p. 1 (my translation).

50 Didi-Huberman, 'Images-pouvoirs ou images-désirs?', pp. 2–3.

51 Félix Guattari, *Chaosmose* (Paris: Éditions Galilée, 1992), p. 127 (my translation).

Also from this series

DISCOURSE 001 Sally Stein *Migrant Mother, Migrant Gender*
DISCOURSE 002 Duncan Forbes *An Interview with Lewis Baltz*
DISCOURSE 003 Jörg Colberg *Photography's Neoliberal Realism*
DISCOURSE 004 C. Fausto Cabrera & Alec Soth *The Parameters of Our Cage*
DISCOURSE 005 Anna Ostoya & Chantal Mouffe *Politics and Passions*
DISCOURSE 006 David Campany & Stanley Wolukau-Wanambwa *Indeterminacy: Thoughts on Time, the Image, and Race(ism)*
DISCOURSE 007 Anouchka Grose & Robert Brewer Young *Uneasy Listening: Notes on Hearing and Being Heard*

Returning to Benjamin
Victor Burgin

First edition published by MACK

Cover, Page 5
Walter Benjamin at the Bibliothèque nationale, Paris, 1937.
Photograph: Gisèle Freund/IMEC/Fonds MCC

Pages 21
WBA 575/29 (old Signature WBA Ms 361). Layout sketch for
the essay on Karl Kraus (1930). Motifs in the third part–Manuscript,
one side.

Design: Morgan Crowcroft-Brown
Copy-edit: Julian Myers
Printed in Germany

ISBN 978-1-913620-91-2
mackbooks.co.uk